Talking to the Wren:

haiku, short verse, and one long poem

by

Mary Harwell Sayler

Talking to the wren,
nesting next to our front porch –

I bring you no harm.

Quick Word to Readers

No matter where we live or in what circumstances, poetry can lift us out of squalor, self-centered perspectives, and apathy! Notice I said "can," not "does," for the power and choice are ultimately up to us.

Nature offers this power too, especially when highlighted by haiku or other poems that give us a touch of surprise, humor, empathy, or beauty we might not have otherwise noticed. Then, as awareness increases, we're encouraged to tend the earth and all of its peoples with closer fellowship, appreciation, and good will.

At least, that's my hope in collecting these poems. And, for me, a symbol that encompasses this lifetime goal is the little wren – one of the tiniest birds but with such a strong, melodic voice!

May the poems in this collection bring blessings to you and everything around you.

Mary Harwell Sayler

www.marysayler.com

Lake Como, Florida, USA

For Bob

and poetry lovers

everywhere

Contents

Tapping into the Aquifer

Haiku cuts rock. Digs
down. Reaches well-water. Lifts
essence into lines.

Summit of All Things

Darkness conspires
to overcome us, but see
how the light points up?
How ancient spires
of buildings build up
toward the light…?

Even the trees climb
the sky with limbs
reaching for evening
light to lift us from
our nocturnal gloom.

Concise Writing Advice

Look to the heron
for focus, eagle for view.
Don't forget the ant.

…

Opening my eyes,
novels, movies, poetry –
Entering your life

…

Reading a dictionary –
Learning the language –
Inventing new words

…

All day I could get
nothing done because poems kept
coming to my mind.

Haiku Alert

Bright wintry morning –
the lily pads shine like glass
flowers on the lake.

...

The sun and wind flash
neon fish upon the pond –
cold swim, bright shining.

...

Dazzling sun flickers
through a wintry pine forest –
thick with disco lights.

...

Low now in the sky,
rays of sunshine claw the trees,
trying to hang on.

Symptom, Not Symbol

The one-eyed heavens
see us encircled in blue
light – cataract moon!

...

Spanish Moss
on an oak tree –
faking a long, long beard

...

On the water's edge,
a great blue heron pretends
to be a statue.

...

Can you feel the chill
of the Anhinga? No oil
to coat its feathers.

...

One sandhill crane sneaks
along our lake – like a teen
tiptoeing past midnight.

At 2 A.M.

The chirp of a bat
startles me by its beauty:
I can see no signs.

...

Black vultures at rest –
surprisingly beautiful –
on the dead branches

...

Three
white birds
in a dead tree

Below the surface
of our small lake, a long log
floats. Alligator!

…

Otters ate the fish
in our little lake. No fresh
alligator food!

…

In Nature, tyrants
have sharp claws, strong teeth, loud mouths,
terrifying eyes.

Morning Music

The sandhill cranes
are on the move, playing
their marimbas.

...

Pink sunrise popping –
Across the pond, a rooster
crows off-key. Morning!

...

On the other side
of the lake, a rooster crows.
The ducks leave a wake.

...

Two sandhill cranes, three
wood storks, a group of egrets:
Postcards on the pond

Chilling

This morning the lake
can see its warm breath, puffing
against the cool air.

…

Haiku, breaking for fog

Warm winter morning –
with fog as thick as white paint
or buttermilk pie

…

Reverberations

On this foggy day,
sounds from everything around
bloom like dandelions.

February in Florida

Everywhere you look
you'll see azaleas blooming.
You'd better like pink!

...

In February,
wild plum trees begin to bloom –
blossoms white as snow.

...

Crepe Myrtle blooming –
Pink clusters everywhere!
Nothing tight-fisted

In an Instant

Each day keeps changing!
Hours dash at breakneck speed.
Calendars give way.

…

Days fly by like bees –
flitting through the calendar,
sticky with honey.

…

Why do I worry?
Birds have such fun winging it.
Lilies freely bloom.

…

Tail of Two Little Bitty Birds

Talking like a WREN,
the voice goes up – like its tail.
SPAR-row's tail goes down.

…

Ideas beginning –
swimming around like goldfish….
Some float to the top.

…

Clouds accumulate thoughts –
stark white, dark grey, purple.
Poems begin to rain.

Spring comes silently –
slow as a caterpillar,
quiet as an owl.

Spring Writes

Nesting birds are text
messaging: *Where r u? What's
happening? Come now!*

…

Tiny little wren –
smaller than magnolia leaves –
texting on the sky!

…

Sandhill cranes nesting
in the shallows one Spring – birds
hatching the water

Garden of Verse

In the failing light,
sun patches the darkened floor –
Poetry flowers.

…

In late afternoon,
yellow Allamanda bloom,
bringing back the light.

…

First hard rain:
The wren abandons her nest
between the stacked chairs.

Finding Giverny off a Sand Road in Rural FL

Monet painted our pond:
wind slurring the water,
lily pads blurred with white
lights against green swirls,
the eye of a cataract sky
awash with Van Gogh's iris.

The lake is alive
with the sound of musical
frogs, bugs, birds, people.

…

Birdcalls moving air!
Stillness springs into action,
then a gentle breeze

…

Two owls arguing
in a territorial
dispute – what a hoot!

After the spring rain,
cool waters inhale the sun –
Fog breathes on the lake

..

Spring rain persisting –
White jasmine bears the heavy
fragrance in its blooms.

…

Pear-shaped
pearl petals –
Magnolia blossoms
cup to catch Spring rain.

Surrounded by lush
woods, fresh water, and wildlife,
we live lavishly.

...

Summer heat in Spring –
The trees seem confused – me too!
My skin is shedding.

....

Wind smudges the lake –
like a pastel painting.
Trees begin to weep.

...

Flexible trees bend
in the wind, but sturdy oaks
are faster to fall.

Finding the Verb for the Trees

Night is a forest –
thick and deep and wide with
the language of trees.

Light comes
with too much dawning on
to listen.

Quietly, the night calls
the pine's perspective, the
oak's endurance, elm's
litheness, maple's
music
made with thick harmony
poured from a core
appearing to be quite golden
but, in reality, as wooden
as a spoon

shaped not
for need but stirring,
amply stirring what
night leaves.

The Evening

Bright orange glowing
through my living room window –
sunset in my house.

cinquain

2 Beneath
4 the neon lights,
6 I catch twilight twinkling
8 where crickets fold their glossy wings
2 and sleep.

Cosmusic

New moon,
quarter-note –
sky song –
key of see

Sentimental Senryu

Many flew the days
we considered to be cheap –
priceless when they're few.

...

Each morning I check
to see if you're still breathing.
Now! I can exhale.

...

In the morning light,
birds begin their lullabies.
Maybe now I'll sleep.

...

If we don't respond,
our alarm clock goes into
hysterical mode.

Every night I try
to paint the sunset with words –
Nothing can express

…

Each sunset adjusts
gradually, light to bright –
like epiphanies.

…

Someone straightened out
the rainbow into a line –
soft summer sunset.

…

The low-lying sun
ignites a cotton blanket
of flammable clouds.

…

Pink flying saucers
trailing across the twilight –
landing in the pond.

Portfolio from the Gulf of Mexico

Beneath the pink fluorescence
of the sun, a flock of terns
collects itself over the water:
waving, undulating, dancing,
shimmering, and shifting their
sky shapes as snake, fish, Ferris
wheel, porpoise, or single strand
of rope. Together, the company
of birds rises, ripples, rolls, and
plunges down to rest on sand
in one great singular body as
though posing for a painting
or an ad for a mutual fund.

Beyond Remembering

Snakes mate:
        a long poetic

dance
        they come together
in loops
        of rope, not love.

Though for a time they intertwine,

they slither on,   past,

        forgetting the dance

that made them

            serpentine

and much too vulnerable.

Still Life

The lake
photographs
the landscape –
a row of trees,
a cabin, the horse
on the water.

Sticky Business

Invisible web –
Spider weaving overhead
Oh, no! A hair net!

...

Armadillo! Knight
in not-so-shining armor
outruns our shy dog.

...

Night sounds. Whippoorwill.
Barking dog. Crickets. My thoughts –
Everything answers.

Road Signs

At work, the cardinal tugs at something I
can't see on the boxwood bush beneath my window.
He's unaware of me, looking on his activity.

Slow-growing upper branches, dark green by summer,
shimmer with the cardinal's movements as though
a playful breeze works through the leaves – also

unseen – like "Men At Work" along an empty
road or like the coming of a line of verse
or the nesting of a poem – without a sign.

Solo Flight

The young cardinal
courted her mirrored image
in the window://pain.

...

Sandhill Crane staring
at himself in the glass doors –
unrequited love

...

Ballerina legs
covered in pencil-thin tights –
graceful Sandhill Cranes

Going with the Creative Flow

rain seeds
water   blooming
puddles   budding
branching
brooks
lakes   streaming
rivulets   burgeoning

rivers
inlets
cays
coves
gulfs
      bays
ocean swells –
Yes!
I want that kind of energy.

Why Blue Haiku?

after discovering Discovery News

Blue whales sound bluer.
Their voices lower oceans
of blue notes wailing.

Likeness

Grey-tan – windblown as
Florida sand, I become
my own true nature.

Reunion

Rain on the lake –
water on water
coming home to rest

Break-dancing

Summer rain flashing
miniature lights on the pond –
breaking into dance

Sound Effects

Suddenly a storm!
Sound effects of thunder – Boom!
Crash! grade c movie

Musicality

Summer rains excite
the frogs on the lake, singing
their raspy praises.

...

Katydids sing in
a canopy of oak trees.
Static fills the leaves.

...

On hot summer nights,
the katydids talk faster,
and I walk slower.

Upholstered

Kudzu leaves its green
drop-cloth over the wooden
furniture of trees.

Mildew

Summer rains painting
trees, grass, porch railings, sidewalks –
everything green!

…

Summer storm passing –
A frog outside our bedroom
grabs a megaphone.

…

Crickets on warm nights
calling one another –
music in their wings

Pardoned

I can understand why we caught fireflies
and kept them in a jar then let them go

(no, not to study their neon niceness, but
because they were so pretty and flashed

near us.) But why did we tie long leashes of
cotton thread around the throats of those poor

squat June bugs before promoting their stalwart
flight? Years later, we accidentally kept

a possum in our compost heap, but not
because we wanted to watch our dog Hannah

leap like a firefly let loose or like a June bug
given its reprieve on a puzzling summer's eve.

A Storm Is Coming!

Summer fireworks flash!
In the distance, cannonballs
break open the sky.

...

The summer weather
has been working up to rain –
writhing, complaining.

...

Gray whale of a cloud
hovering over the lake
belly flopping – rain!

....

Deluge!
Sheets of rain
cannot be measured
in meters
or inches
but thread count.

Lightning pries the sky
open like an oyster shell.
Hard rain falls like pearls.

…

Hot. Heavy. The air
dangles its electric cords –
plugging into earth.

…

Electricity
cracks the sky like a walnut –
each half trembling.

…

The heavy storm breaks,
telling us to lighten up.
Oh, how fresh the air!

The day the sky fell
into the lake – no harm done –
serene symmetry.

...

Patterns of raindrops
on the window draw moons, stars,
galaxies on glass.

...

Letting go of rain,
life drops unexpectedly –
sadness, joy, new growth.

Precipitation

i.
clouds rise like homemade bread
mother can you hear me

inside the rain
you proclaim: you're weird

i'm not
i say
showing you
my poems removing
most articles
of clothing

ii.
she likes paris plastered
with culture

i like talking to you
in torrents

iii.
a half-drowned chameleon
turns into
rain

Lizards have clothing
colored for each occasion –
fence post, tree – not me!

...

Lizard in the house
immobilized by crayons –
choosing what to wear

...

On the horizon
puffy white chef's hats arise –
summer sky cooking

Buzz

A bee paused mid-air –
bright yellow helicopter!
Summer stares at me.

...

Cocoon
of childhood –
time fluttering by –
butterflies swarming

...

Butterflies – paper
white, paper thin – stout beach winds:
Oh, such stamina!

Beach Scenes: Folk Art from the Fifth Floor

I.

From the oceanfront condo where we like to stay, we watch
the water fluctuate the shore with the thin insinuation of a line.
Ever changing, nothing ever does, or so it seems when dreams
have wakened, hard, and lost their hold. A fish crow flaps its
wings in patterns reminiscent of a Native American dance then
flies offstage from our broad balcony view. Do you think we'll be
hard-bodied again like that beach-walking couple below us,
holding hands? I hope not! I don't care to sculpt myself into a
more elaborately concocted shell than sits on any ocean shelf. You
look good to me – with natural lines and moods as ever changing
as expressions from the sea.

II.

We've only been here an hour and already the aqua colors have
altered to grayed blue-green on the horizon and grayed yellow-
green toward the shore. Up high like this on the fifth floor, an
obvious metaphor arises as sudsy waves wash against a scrub-
board of wet sand. But when has anyone last seen a hand-held
washing board, much less known it's used for scrubbing clothes?

From an airplane flying over rocky mountains, the view is much
the same, but here, smudged peaks and treeless ridges of beige
and charcoal lines bear the footprints of water giants – whole
families of them, wearing denim shorts and stepping over sand-

cliffs and watery valleys into the soft wreck of a sandcastle.
III.
On the horizon, sailboats hoist their teepees
to tag the tongues where sky and water meet.

IV.
Here is a rule to keep: Do not shake a blanket
into a sleeper's space nor into the face of wind.

V.
Why is that woman lying on the sand without even a stitch
of beach towel to stop the grit and fleas? Aren't some things
uncomfortable at any age?

My neck hurts from hanging over pages to see what my pencil
does: The water-scalloped sand is the broad back of an oyster
shell, seldom seen on this shoreline, and sea oats lean into the
wind like striking snakes.

A seagull hovers on the horizon, sailing its kite
wings without a string, and everything else unwinds
as the sun begins the nightly rounds of pardoning.

VI.
Here's another rule: Do not trust an ink pen to anyone
with closed eyes: The ocean sounds like a mountain
scene with waterfalls and gusts of wind or a speeding
train in a tunnel or the roaring applause at the end of a
Broadway play or the cheering crowd at a high school
football game or a fire raging in a pine forest or an oil
well set aflame or the tires sloshing in a drenching rain
with traffic warnings whistling from every life-guardian.

VII.

Outside ourselves, haiku happens:

Moving frontward, side
ways, with a clear bubble top:
all-terrain sand crab

VIII.

And every person on the beach becomes a poem.

IX.

As the sun sifts into the sand, we pay our tab for a rum
runner we somewhat shared (yes, I took the better part),
then we stroll along a shoreline loosely scrolled by the
last low tide into an ancient manuscript. On our left, we
pass an old motel, hardbound with stories, yet the place
still stands its ground. Perhaps it's overtaxed and written
over with graffiti but, to the right

                                        the sea.

Head down in the wind
birds hang, wooden, on the line –
weather-worn clothespins.

…

Outside my window,
a bird is mimicking *you* –
whistling like a bird!

…

Music in Autumn –
woodpeckers chuckle, crows caw,
dogs bark: Percussion!

Heavy autumn air
breaks with the shriek of a hawk –
prelude to horror!

...

A murder of crows
fighting for territory –
Gangsters. Tree thugs. Crime.

...

Debris on the lake
floating like dead animals
makes me feel so sad.

...

Stretched across our door
lay the black-brown scaly skin
a snake left behind.

Wild turkey and chick,
peacefully pecking dry seeds,
stroll through our back yard.

...

An aerial show!
Over the arc of oak trees –
six buzzards circling

...

Foggy Fall morning –
The sun is a silver coin
polished by grey clouds.

..

See how old I feel!
In Autumn, the night light draws
a moth to my shine.

I'm mad at squirrels!
Don't they know how much it costs
to fix what they've chewed?

…

Squirrels love to climb
Maggie our magnolia tree,
pilfering her pods.

…

Squirrels pelt our roof
with magnolia pods. Summer
leaves us with a bang!

Do Not Use the Word *Bury* in This Poem

Squirrels shop
the earth. Moles
have malls. Robins extract
worms known for aeration.

Elatedly, archeologists
belatedly uncover
a level of ash
from an ancient city
razed beyond repair.

How did we get there?

The dark earth keeps deep
secrets only amblers know.

Cushy Casita Scene: On Vacation

The birds seem bigger here,
and squirrels the size of cats

scat across the golden sand
into a bramble-branched

ravine. So far I've seen
a Gambel's Quail, a spotted

thrush, a hummingbird, a
"wild boar," and the tracks

of a bobcat, adventuring
here, near our rented door.

Walking to a Mall in Arizona

Purple lupine
blooms along the trail.
Gambel's Quail amble
across pebble-packed sand.
A cotton-tailed hare
stares, unblinking, where
I stop and stand at dusk
to watch a javelina hold me
in its peculiar peccarian sites
between uplifted
tusks.

No rain! Shrinking lake –
crows walking on mud-margins,
Sandhill cranes nesting

…

Cattails drying up –
Where have all the showers gone?
Mud flats flowering

…

Rain drops on dry leaves,
sounding like Morse Code clicking –

I get the message.

…

Days crisp with color –
Leaves falling from their heavy
burden of beauty.

…

Paisley patterns perfected
inside the polished rock

Wind and water shape
magnificent mountain peaks.

Air and spirit rise!

...
Beautiful the eyes
who see God in all places
through every face.

...

Your faith – smaller than
a mustard seed – branches out.
Much shade! Many nests!

Swaths of orange-pink
float on the water's surface.
Earth and Heaven meet.

...

At sunset, tree frogs
herald the evening light -
a purple frenzy

...

Angels on the pond
little searchlights blinking –
Oh! Is someone lost?

Ruah

Wind rushes across
the lake like a wave of praise
stirring the waters.

…

Listening to night –
with its call and responses –
I await God's voice.

…

In every season –
Thunder! and the still, small Voice!
God is All in all.

Acknowledgements

"Black Vultures at Rest" included in "Saying More Than You Say" on the Poetry Editor blog

"Bright wintry morning" published in *Written River*

"Butterflies – paper" in *Written River*

"Cinquain" in *Writer's Gazette*

"Cocoon of childhood" accepted for the *Horizon: Haiku Anthology* by Cyberwit

"Crickets on Warm Nights" accepted for the *Horizon: Haiku Anthology* by Cyberwit

"Every night I try" on Micropoetry.com

"In the morning light" posted in "Revising for Sound and Sense" on the Poetry Editor blog

"Lightning pries the sky" accepted for the *Horizon: Haiku Anthology* by Cyberwit

"Lizard in my house" published in *Written River*

"Nature's Irony" included in "Saying More Than You Say" on the Poetry Editor blog

"On the horizon" on Micropoetry.com

"Outside my window" accepted for the *Horizon: Haiku Anthology* by Cyberwit

"Reverberations" on author's page of Hiraeth Press

"Spanish Moss" in *Failed Haiku*

"Sticky Business" on Micropoetry.com

"The rusty needles " included in "Observation Makes the Poem" on the Poetry Editor blog

Poems from the book *Living in the Nature Poem*
(published by Hiraeth, now out of print)

"At 2 A.M."

"Finding Giverny off a Sand Road in Rural FL"; also in *Wild Violet*

"Haiku Alert"; also in *Haiku Journal*

"Likeness"

"Spring Rites"